GW00759250

THE ULTIMATE VILLANELLE COLLECTION

Edited by

Heather Killingray

First published in Great Britain in 1998 by
POETRY NOW
1-2 Wainman Road, Woodston,
Peterborough, PE2 7BU
Telephone (01733) 230746
Fax (01733) 230751

Copyright Contributors 1998

HB ISBN 0 75430 476 0
SB ISBN 0 75430 477 9

FOREWORD

Although we are a nation of poetry writers we are accused of not reading poetry and not buying poetry books: after many years of listening to the incessant gripes of poetry publishers, I can only assume that the books they publish, in general, are books that most people do not want to read.

Poetry should not be obscure, introverted, and as cryptic as a crossword puzzle: it is the poet's duty to reach out and embrace the world.

The world owes the poet nothing and we should not be expected to dig and delve into a rambling discourse searching for some inner meaning.

The reason we write poetry (and almost all of us do) is because we want to communicate: an ideal; an idea; or a specific feeling. Poetry is as essential in communication, as a letter; a radio; a telephone, and the main criteria for selecting the poems in this anthology is very simple: they communicate.

A *villanelle* is a poem of 19 lines arranged in 6 stanzas. The first five stanzas have three lines each (tercets) and the last stanza has four lines (a quatrain). The first and last lines of the first stanza serve as refrains which are repeated in turn, throughout the poem - until the last stanza where they come together to form the last two lines of the poem.

This villanelle collection was a result of our founder, Ian Walton's workshop. It includes some of the best villanelle attempts that we have come across to date.

Numerous subjects have encountered the villanelle experience and serve as a useful guide to those who lack knowledge, or have an interest in the poetic form of a villanelle.

Read it from cover to cover, you will enjoy this villanelle experience and I am sure that you will soon be picking up a pen and trying it yourself.

CONTENTS

TOO LATE

You realise, now that it is too late -
Now that your life is nearly at its end -
Things do not always come to those who wait.

You've spent your life, complaining of your fate,
Until you've ended up without a friend.
You realise, now that it is too late,

Now that you are alone, and in this state,
With cancer spreading, no more time to spend,
Things do not always come to those who wait.

You didn't think of writing your own slate.
Life was too treacherous to comprehend.
You realise, now that it is too late.

You wanted sons, and wealth, and silver plate,
A rich husband, on whom you could depend.
Things do not always come to those who wait.

Your legacy is bitterness and hate,
Because, when life's gales blew, you couldn't bend.
You realise, now that it is too late,
Things do not always come to those who wait.

Laurel Wingfield

BY THE JEWISH MEMORIAL IN AMSTERDAM, (NOOR AUSCHWITZ)

Among the ashes and the grime
By that stone we stood
Each holding the narrow tube of time.

Though frozen tears were wasted and sighed
And English voices said they could
Among the ashes and the grime.

I saw an opaque prayer fly from someone blind
The souls of dying children made of wood
Each holding the narrow tube of time.

A mocking German soldier began to shine,
85 thousand Jews were shut down like a hood
Among the ashes and the grime.

The same tram tracks unveiled the crime
Dividing a city from bad to good
Each holding the narrow tube of time.

A crying father and a child kicking a chime
One saying *Kaddish** because he should
Among the ashes and the grime
Each holding the narrow tube of time.

   *(*Kaddish is memorial prayer for the dead)*

Andy Strowman

THE LIGHTHOUSE

Lonely standing on its rock
Landmark for the sailors' eyes
Vivid white, quite a shock!

A block of granite, a flock
Of seabirds resting on its sides
Their eyes, alert, a cock!

The lighthouse-keeper felt the knock
When the pounding sea smashed
Against the solid surface
What a shock!

Watching from his perch on the rock
He gazed with heartfelt terror
His mouth was all a-cock!

A submarine surfaced what a mock
For his startled eyes full of fear
A sub had never been before
What a shock!

Marston is here early to relieve you Trock
Come on board we have news for you,
Trock couldn't answer he was in great shock!

The lighthouse stood firmly on the rock
The keeper had been cat-napping a lot!
No submarine could be seen,
His mind had gone a-cock!

Alma Montgomery Frank

THERE IS AN END

There is an end to the long winter's sleep.
After dormant winter comes bursting spring.
Let us awake, rejoice, refuse to weep.

Across the frosty field the roe deer leap.
Aroused is every hibernating thing.
There is an end to the long winter's sleep.

Daily advance all things that stir and creep.
Early dawn invites early birds to sing.
Let us awake, rejoice, refuse to weep.

In the still pond frogspawn dropped in a heap
Swells and grows, little tails developing.
There is an end to the long winter's sleep.

At last the cuckoo comes, a tryst to keep,
With strange abandoning of its offspring.
Let us awake, rejoice, refuse to weep.

Over hazy field, gliding, swooping deep
The swallows gather food while on the wing.
There is an end to the long winter's sleep.
Let us awake, rejoice, refuse to weep.

Ardis Gaylor

CHOICE

Too many gods there are.
Which of them is best to choose?
O god afar!

'All are par, are par,'
Say Hindus with their deities profuse.
Too many gods there are.

'We have no bar, no bar,'
Say Moslems, who are anti-booze.
O god afar!

'Think of the scar, the scar,'
Say Christians, mindful of the cross's screws.
Too many gods there are.

'No war, no war, no war,'
Say Buddhists with their loving views.
O god afar!

'Chosen we are, we are,'
Say Hebrew scripts of ancient Jews.
Too many gods there are.
O god afar!

Charles W Brown

FRIENDSHIP

We're here for you each day
The future holds no threat
We will not go away

Have faith, for come what may
You are not beaten yet
We're here for you each day

You're lonely, sad you say
You're caught within a net
We will not go away

We're here, and here we'll stay
We owe you such a debt
We're here for you each day

Together we will pray
Though dark the night as jet
We will not go away

So all your fears allay
And please do not forget
We're here for you each day
We will not go away

Cathie Bridger

On Wings Of Mind

Be still all you devils and let me lie,
I need a peace to contemplate.
My mind has wings wherewith to fly.

This time-waste stream of endless cry
Aborts my will to gravitate.
Be still all you devils and let me lie.

The air above, unfathomed azure sky
Spurs on my brain to activate.
My mind has wings whereon to fly.

You simper on, persistent pry
To hamper need to levitate.
Be still all you devils and let me lie.

The birds are there, I hear their cry,
Perhaps by lesson I can imitate.
My mind has wings wherewith to fly.

At least I am worth another try,
An effort one more time to infiltrate.
Be still all you devils and let me lie,
My mind has wings wherewith to fly.

John Tomlinson

THE GRANDCHILDREN ARE GROWING

It's quiet now at close of day
Childish laughter echoes here
And memories of joyful play

Special guests who came to stay
And filled our world with love and cheer
The children shared our lives today

The magic of a kiss a childish way
Most precious touch - a silver tear
And memories of joyful play

Powdered limbs and knee-scarred play
Sunny fragrant hours when they appear
The children shared our lives today

Chocolate sticky to rugby muddy day
Finger paints or drawings we hold dear
And memories of joyful play

We've 'swum' a mead of summer hay
Scratched for worms to fish the weir
And memories of joyful play
The children shared our lives today

John Burton

CARING HEARTS

We who have a care
Can see where it does good
It flourishes everywhere.

A good turn I declare
Will benefit all eventually
We who have a care.

If a happy heart is there -
It is joy in contact we know
It flourishes everywhere.

A task done unaware
Can surprise give content
We who have a care.

Feel free of love's despair
This silken thread of emotion
It flourishes everywhere.

He who ventures today
May good of life be part
We who have a care
It flourishes everywhere.

Victoria Joan Theedam

THE TREE WAS THERE

The tree was there in summer sun last year,
And mayflies danced where laughing children play
In golden glow, the memories so dear.

The innocents were guarded from all fear,
No sombre shadows till the close of day,
The tree was there in summer sun last year.

At early morn the song thrush did appear,
To sing amongst the willows and the bay
In golden glow, the memories so dear.

Those happy days when skies were blue and clear
And Flora dressed in all her fine array,
The tree was there in summer sun last year.

The feller's ruthless hand was almost near
To take the weeping willow in decay,
In golden glow, the memories so dear,

And I could only shed a silent tear,
Lamenting for the boughs of leafy spray;
The tree was there in summer sun last year,
In golden glow, the memories so dear.

A J Don

THE CARER

I cannot always stay,
The house is dead and still!
As they often pass away . . .

Broken bones, hair turned grey,
Time to give out a pill!
I cannot always stay.

Broken minds, tooth decay,
My duty to fulfil!
As they often pass away . . .

I always kneel to pray
When there's a deathly shrill!
I cannot always stay.

I love them every day,
But nature comes to kill!
As they often pass away . . .

There's pain for me today,
In my heart there's a chill!
I cannot always stay,
As they often pass away . . .

Denise Russell

SUN

O sun be in my heart,
O sun be in my soul,
And in my every part.

Help me now to chart
My voyage to *your* soul,
O sun be in my heart.

From darkness to depart,
From sin and evil whole,
And in my every part.

O strengthen me to start
My flight from death's dark toll,
O sun be in my heart,

And save me from the dart
Of old age in my poll,
And in my every part.

In risen Christ to start
Again in different role,
O sun be in my heart
And in my every part.

Ira Foxwell

MEASURED THOUGHTS

Her dreams now all but dust, decayed
Exhausted, she's no energy left to fight,
Her thoughts she measured, balanced and weighed.

She watched them fall as she sat and prayed,
Enlightenment needed to end her plight,
Her dreams now all but dust, decayed.

Nerves are shattered, so badly frayed,
How could he steal away into the night,
Her thoughts she measured, balanced and weighed.

Sitting quietly, emotions her sanity slayed,
How could she have been deprived of foresight,
Her dreams now all but dust, decayed.

Desperately she wishes, that he had stayed,
Her insecure tension, pulls her insides tight,
Her thoughts she measured, balanced and weighed.

Shock arises, the realisation, so delayed,
None of this can she put right,
Her dreams now all but dust, decayed,
Her thoughts she measured, balanced and weighed.

Elaine Hawkins

FOOD IN MY BELLY

I have food in my belly.
I have a nice warm bed,
And a video and telly.

Are you poor! Are you silly!
Don't you know I'm well fed.
I have food in my belly.

I can hear. I can see.
There's an electric bed,
And a video and telly.

With trainers, to suit me.
Red/green hair on my head.
I have food in my belly.

I have a car - or three.
I have silks on my bed,
And a video and telly.

Every week, it's lottery.
It's the mortgage I dread.
I have food in my belly,
And a video and telly.

Doreen King

As Time Goes By

What maketh thou, as time goes by?
Dost thou meanly through life flee?
Be wise, time will soon come to die!

Friendships, trust, you must now tie,
or lonely fate, dull life for thee.
What maketh thou, as time goes by?

So smile at all, and cheerful cry,
they will respond, nature does decree.
Be wise, time will soon come to die.

I know these things, this I can verify,
days can be scented, as sweet pea.
What maketh thou, as time goes by.

In confidence go forth, don't be shy,
let now your heart roam pastures free.
Be wise, time will soon come to die.

Now it's time, for now my end is nigh,
My thoughts and love I leave with thee.
What maketh thou as time goes by?
Be wise, time will soon come to die.

Howden Brook

AUTUMN

As trees prepare for winter's icy sleep
Red squirrels sway on fragile beech trapeze
And tattered leaves lie rotting in a heap.

To hibernation lazy hedgehogs creep
Limp blooms provide no pollen for the bees
As trees prepare for winter's icy sleep.

The grain is ripe the time has come to reap,
Damp fungus thrives on sodden bark of trees
And tattered leaves lie rotting in a heap.

The willows shiver round the pond and weep
While gentle ripples soon will stop and freeze
As trees prepare for winter's icy sleep.

Springtime lambs now sheep no longer leap
Fat lazy cows sedately take their ease
And tattered leaves lie rotting in a heap.

Pine cones and mosses now form a carpet deep
Beneath the woodland giants' rugged knees
As trees prepare for winter's icy sleep
And tattered leaves lie rotting in a heap.

Mary Rea

Party At Three

It is my birthday today
I am having a party at three
Please come and stay.

I live at Four Tree Way
Come and be with me
It is my birthday today.

We are getting a takeaway
It will be a wonderful tea
Please come and stay.

Come straight away
With a plate of food on your knee
It is my birthday today.

It is a nice sunny day
It will be a sight to see
Please come and stay.

Others are coming to play
A happy time it will be
It is my birthday today
Please come and stay.

Alan Hatton

I'M SCARED

(Dedicated to my friends Ann and Paul. So glad for you)

How can this be happening to me?
Whilst having a bath found a lump in my chest.
This is not what I thought would be.

Hospitalised, not far from Poole Quay
Surgery, pain, it's done, home to rest.
How can this be happening to me?

I don't want to die, want friends round to tea
It's like a black cloud, can't eat, have no zest.
This is not what I thought would be.

Not sure of my future, worried, me more than he.
Friends rally round, jesting, doing their best.
How can this be happening to me?

How long, how soon, D-Day Friday for me,
Worrying, wondering, in this world I'll detest.
This is not what I thought would be.

Thumbs up, she's smiling, I'm totally free
It's benign, yes, in my future I'll invest.
How can this be happening to me.
This is not what I thought would be.

B M Hurll

ON THE ROAD

Driving through the night
Unzipping the cat's eyes
Wishing, wishing, for the light

While you were so polite
Asking was it wise
Driving through the night

Although it's still not quite
Time for morning's sun to rise
I'm wishing, wishing, for that light

Already missing sheer delight
Those mutual sensual highs
Driven through the night

Could it all be simply spite
Can't bear to hear dark lies
Wishing, wishing, for some light

Enduring what's not right
Knowing that love does die
Driving through the night
Wishing, wishing, for the light

Nick Colton

BEYOND THE LAKE

Beyond the lake on light tiptoe
Blithe meadow nymph in silken dress,
Her graceful form did sprightly go.

Melodic sounds with soft outflow
Her joyous song of happiness,
Beyond the lake on light tiptoe.

Enchantment pure my heart's flambeau,
Skipping along with great finesse
Her graceful form did sprightly go.

While splendour reigned love did bestow
Her seeds of love without caress,
Beyond the lake on light tiptoe.

Emotion came with tears to show
She'd won my heart and with success,
Her graceful form did sprightly go.

My heart was touched by sublime glow,
And so my friends I now confess,
Beyond the lake on light tiptoe
Her graceful form did sprightly go.

Peter James O'Rourke

THE ECHO OF YOUR CALL

When day is done and shadows fall
Peaceful is the silent night as
I hear the echo of your call.

Days are endless and, I spend my nights
Counting the stars that gaze through my window
When day is done and shadows fall.

The restless moon goes sailing by
As I listen to distant church bells chime, and
I hear the echo of your call.

Golden memories are forever mine,
But oh so lonely are the nights
When day is done and shadows fall.

Time goes by and the world stands still
As I dream of the happiness we once shared, then
I hear the echo of your call.

My thoughts are with you night and day
And I raise my glass to your memory.
When day is done and shadows fall
I hear the echo of your call.

Phyllis R Harvey

In The Still Of The Night

Heed not too much those niggling doubts tremendous,
Tossing and turning in the light of dawn,
Besetting weary mind ta'en all too credulous.

As others' needs recalled as quite horrendous
Dismiss the errant thoughts that then are born,
Heed not too much those niggling doubts tremendous.

Forget the twists and turns of fortune, androgynous,
Or yet high hopes that could appear forlorn;
Besetting weary mind ta'en all too credulous.

'Tis well to nurture instincts most gregarious,
'Though you may find in some full flavour shorn,
Heed not too much those niggling doubts tremendous.

Remember not all needless words nefarious
That, having heard, gives you most cause to mourn,
Besetting weary mind ta'en all too credulous.

Let Lethe bring to you her gift stupendous,
May Morpheus embrace before the morn,
Heed not too much those niggling doubts tremendous,
Besetting weary mind ta'en all too credulous.

Mary Ryan

MODERATELY GREEN

When trees mark time upon attendant hills
and mixers spew their breeze-block pollen out -
this is the time to note the nation's ills!

Down in some valley hear the timber mills
sing, as their pyramids stand guard without
and trees mark time upon attendant hills.

Haven't you seen how clean a highway kills?
Yet; while life still survives within the grout,
this is the time to note the nation's ills.

Not everything the seismic team reveals
is passed on high. There *may* be oil about
when trees mark time upon attendant hills

- and there may not! The 'green' men study stills
and scream 'Ignore the bloody oilman's clout.
This is the time to note the nation's ills!'

We moderates must balance well our skills
and our lives - but when timber stocks run out
as trees mark time upon attendant hills,
this is the time to note the nation's ills.

Brian Willis

A WORLD AT PEACE

Mankind is yearning for a world at peace,
When sweet perfume of love is everywhere;
Respect and trust then make all anger cease.

When friendship is no longer on a lease
Which could expire with each ensuing year,
Mankind is yearning for a world at peace.

Sharp practice can goad sellers prone to fleece,
So fairness shines to keep base cheapness clear;
Respect and trust then make all anger cease.

When ironing you always press to crease
And obliterate wrinkles which are there;
Mankind is yearning for a world at peace

There's a dour noun, unhappy, stark: decease;
Loved ones have gone and cannot reappear;
Respect and trust then make all anger cease.

The world's own conduct must be its to police,
To rid from states and races, abject fear;
Mankind is yearning for a world at peace
Respect and trust then make all anger cease.

Dennis Marshall

FLY INTO THE FRAY

Fly bravely into the battle fray
May good fortune follow you;
As sky is in disarray.

All earthly colours green to grey,
Mix with midday blue;
Turn fast he slips away.

Follow in, make the villain pay,
Aim your Browning true;
As the sky is in disarray.

He banks to port in battle play,
Stick to him like glue;
Turn fast he slips away.

One good burst is it night or day,
He's hit, bullets he's due;
As the sky is in disarray.

Battle over for another day
Villain gone it's true;
As the sky is in disarray,
Turn fast he slips, away.

Peter M McCulloch

I Wait

I wait awake again
The middle of the night
For you to think of me and call.

But I await in vain . . .
I must extinguish light.
You have not thought of me at all.

Tomorrow at my work
With you in mind all day,
Maybe the coming evening you will call!

True, yesterday we talked,
That's gone and far away.
Today you will not think of me at all?

I would call you
But then I'd worry
If you're not in to answer to my call.

Then, doubts anew,
And feeling sorry,
That you don't think of me at all.

Just now we talked,
Yet seems like whole long days
Since I've rushed, in answer to your call.
In lonely silence now . . . you do not think of me at all!

Elena Hopkins

The Humble Servant

My friend who was a brother
To those of us in need,
Gave his life to serve another.

What shall I tell you Mother?
That we did not heed,
My friend who was a brother.

He was unlike any other
Obedient in the deed,
Gave his life to serve another.

We talked but did not bother
Of the hungry he did feed,
My friend who was a brother.

In prayer he would rather
Be alone, he sowed the seed,
Gave his life to serve another.

He asked us through the Father
To follow in his lead.
My friend who was a brother
Gave his life to serve another.

Cynthia Beaumont

ON HAPPINESS

Real happiness in life depends
On satisfying cherished dreams;
On steady nerves achieving ends

On making light of adverse trends
On seeing through important schemes
Real happiness in life depends

The soul uplifts when mind extends
And enters into upward streams
On steady nerves achieving ends

On temperament that never bends
Towards pursuit of wild extremes
Real happiness in life depends

Conform when instinct recommends
Concede when inner-self esteems
On steady nerves achieving ends

Exciting pleasure rather tends
To fade away - as lesser themes
Real happiness in life depends
On steady nerves, achieving ends.

Jack Conway

PLAYING HOST

The fox stopped by to feed last night
As she had done most times before
As the dark was filled with light.

For she had learned to trip the light
To find the food; to raid the store.
The fox stopped by to feed last night.

And so she snuffed the plants in sight.
We saw the snails crushed in her jaw
As the dark was filled with light.

Then just as we had hoped she might
She found the scraps placed near the door.
The fox stopped by to feed last night.

In darkened room we watched despite
The urge to speak; to move forbore,
As the dark was filled with light.

And then I moved and lost the fight.
She heard. She fled. With haste she tore.
The fox stopped by to feed last night
As the dark was filled with light.

Bob Jones

THE RIDDLE OF LOVE

Since love lies bleeding in my heart again,
And puts my soul-spent ecstasies to flight,
I try once more to rationalise the pain:

Perhaps it's through the sorrowful refrain
Of songs which set the old desire alight
That love lies bleeding in my heart again;

Or is it but the embers that remain
When life's refulgence passes into night?
I try once more to rationalise the pain.

It goes against the rationalising grain
Of seeing, knowing that the heart was right
That love lies bleeding in my heart again.

A riddle that torments the fevered brain
Is love in this strange, tantalising light.
I try once more to rationalise the pain,

To make the contours of love's mystery plain,
The lamp of her eternal being bright.
Since love lies bleeding in my heart again,
I try once more to rationalise the pain.

S H Smith

CAMOMILE LAWN

(For Jyrki Arthur Ilmari Seppänen/
George Arthur Ilmari Smithson)

'Pon a camomile lawn,
The Shah sits alone,
'Midst a warm Persian dawn.

With a look all forlorn,
He doth wail and bemoan;
'Pon a camomile lawn.

Beard clipp'd and shorn,
His heart beats like stone:
'Midst a warm Persian dawn.

Robes ragged and torn,
'Fore a grand Peacock Throne:
'Pon a camomile lawn.

Yet one so high born,
Must now die on his own:
'Midst a warm Persian dawn.

Soon cometh the morn',
The Shah's chill'd to the bone:
'Pon a camomile lawn,
'Midst a warm Persian dawn.

David Brasier

IF I COULD NOT SEE

I would miss so much if I could not see
Shadows on the grass, cream clouds racing by
The swaying branches of the cedar tree.

Small silver tinsel eucalyptus leaves
Glinting in winter's overcast skies
I would miss so much if I could not see.

The heron in the shallows, lazy bees
Round the vine, flashing, brilliant dragonflies.
The swaying branches of the cedar tree.

Cascading fireworks spontaneous, free
Silver stars break the night falling to die
I would miss so much if I could not see.

Cowrie shells and driftwood washed by the sea
Tiny pearls' treasure trove bare at low tide
The swaying branches of the cedar tree.

Your smiling face sometimes laughing at me
The look in your eyes that can make me cry
I would miss so much if I could not see
The swaying branches of the cedar tree.

Jan Ingram McCaffery

LAST TIME I LEFT

Last time I left, you were asleep in bed
and I was jealous of that early morning doze
with not a thought of what might lie ahead.

In front, a mile away, the tail lights flicker red.
The embers brighten as the traffic slows;
last time I left, you were asleep in bed.

Carriageway repairs - the yellow notice said.
So, cars and trucks are corralled into rows,
as now I wonder what might lie ahead.

Far, far away, the snaking line seems dead -
how serious the hold-up is, one never knows.
Last time I left, you were asleep in bed.

Is there a chance to take another road instead?
You're never quite sure where the slip-road goes . . .
Last time I left you, you were asleep in bed
and now I wonder what might lie ahead.

Trevor Millum

GOSSAMER, POISED ON A STEM

Gossamer. Poised on a stem.
Motionless. By all unseen.
Stillness. Telling it must leave.

No movement. No feeling is shown.
Time passes in its own way.
Gossamer. Poised on a stem.

Summer shared. Pain and sweet joy.
Reeds lying partly submerged.
Stillness. Telling it must leave.

Hold nature's hand for a time.
Nothing shows. All knowledge gone.
Gossamer. Poised on a stem.

Security but for how long?
Breezes grow cold as in grave.
Gossamer. Poised on a stem.
Stillness. Telling it must leave.

Barbara Goode

VILLANELLE

I like my house, although it's old,
As long as it is sound and dry
I can't agree it should be sold.

Strong oaken pegs the framework hold,
And though the gables look awry
I like my house, although it's old.

It's stood while centuries have rolled
And still attracts the passers-by,
I can't agree it should be sold.

It's quickly warmed and seldom cold,
So comfortable, it makes me sigh,
'I like my house, although it's old.'

The building's sound, so I've been told,
It suits me well, and that is why
I can't agree it should be sold.

What memories its walls enfold!
I hope to stay here till I die.
I like my house, although it's old,
I can't agree it should be sold.

Betty Byrom

BY THE RIVER TRENT

By the River Trent, where I spend my days
Reliving youth, and biding time.
Our paths through life have many ways.

I see Clifton pit, now in a haze
Of memory; blackening man with grime,
By the River Trent where I spend my days.

By old Wilford bridge, I'd swim and laze,
Playing truant, when it was a crime.
Our paths through life have many ways.

To cut a bulrush, was a phase
In swamps, where newts played, so sublime.
By the River Trent where I spend my days.

I see old streets, with horse and drays.
A grandmother clock, that didn't chime.
Our paths through life have many ways.

The staff at Bosworth school I praise.
They taught me how to write a line.
By the River Trent where I spend my days.

My friends at school, they would amaze
With saucy wit and cheeky rhyme.
Our paths through life have many ways.

A life is time we can't rephrase
There is much regret for what I am.
By the River Trent where I spend my days.

Was old 'Meadow' life an act of plays?
With all the ghosts of bygone times.
Our paths through life have many ways.

I think of love; was it a craze,
I find you, in my every line.
By the River Trent where I spend my days.
Our paths through life have many ways.

Richard Cluroe

WE WILL MEET AGAIN ONE DAY

You went away
And it does seem
We will meet again one day.

'It was an accident' I hear a voice say
I wanted to scream
You went away.

You were my light and ray
We were a great team
We will meet again one day.

You looked peaceful as you lay
It felt like a dream,
You went away.

Last respects they pay
And it does seem
We will meet again one day.

I think of you every day
And think of what could have been
You went away
We will meet again one day.

Clare Field (16)

WHERE IS MY DAD?

Where is my Dad?
I ask you every day,
Was he very bad?

It makes me sad
Do I have to pay,
Where is my Dad?

Was he so mad
As to stay away?
Was he very bad?

Was he a cad
When he went astray?
Where is my Dad?

Is it just a fad,
A game to play?
Was he very bad?

I would be glad
If he came to stay.
Was he very bad?
Where is my Dad?

Carol Venus

THE VILLAGE BY THE VOLCANO

Give us some idea
When you want us to leave
We are trembling with fear

Our homes that we hold dear
Are those we must leave
Give us some idea

The air smells very queer
That you can't deceive
We are trembling with fear

The rumble means death is near
Will someone our transport problems relieve?
Give us some idea

Move out time is almost here
Why should we have to grieve
We are trembling with fear

The situation is almost clear
In our village by the volcano
Give us some idea
We are trembling with fear

P Edwards

WHERE CAN THE COWSLIPS BE?

Oh where, oh where can the cowslips be,
Lemon bells I picked in yesteryear,
Those wee small flowers so beloved by me?

I've sought in meadows but cannot see
Those golden parasols I held dear,
Oh where, oh where can the cowslips be?

They danced together so prettily,
They are gone, forever, now I fear,
Those wee small flowers so beloved by me.

Childhood innocence, I picked in glee,
Now their absence makes me shed a tear,
Oh where, oh where can the cowslips be?

They yielded their nectar to the bee.
Did the roads and transport come too near
Those wee small flowers so beloved by me?

I regret that they were forced to flee,
That I will never see them, I fear,
Oh where, oh where can the cowslips be,
Those wee small flowers so beloved by me?

Pat Heppel

THE SINKING SHIP

I will sail alone,
As the navigator is gone, and the ship is sinking down,
I am afraid to sail home.

In the darkness, very late in the night,
In the mornings, at the day's dawn,
I will sail alone.

In the hottest summer, in the coldest winter,
As the ship's engine's sounds drone,
I am afraid to sail home.

Who will sail with me, now for good you have gone,
The ship is empty, as I am just alone and drawn,
I will sail alone.

You deserted the ship, when it was sailing home,
In the middle of the ocean, you have left me to drown,
I am afraid to sail home.

Together we sailed, now you have left the captain on his own,
To sail in the thick of the dark mist, as
I will sail alone,
I am afraid to sail home.

Jonathan A Sande

TIME

One second, one minute, one hour, one day,
  Tired old so frail, vibrant young, no fear,
Time races on from soft snow til' fresh hay.

The strangest phenomenon or a year gone astray?
  Moulding each person from pauper to peer,
One second, one minute, one hour, one day.

Like a prancing predator pouncing its prey,
  A life minus time producing a tear,
Time races on from soft snow til' fresh hay.

No stillness or stopping for joy or dismay,
  Remembering the good times seems so clear,
One second, one minute, one hour, one day.

A priceless possession we lose to decay,
  The adding to life in abundance, so dear,
Time races on from soft snow til' fresh hay.

Our God the only one to have a say,
  As mortals we can but only adhere,
One second, one minute, one hour, one day,
  Time races on from soft snow til' fresh hay.

Martin Crawley

THE SOURCE OF SWEET REGRET

She was just someone I once met;
We talked for a brief hour or two,
But she's a source of sweet regret.

Her memory in my mind is set.
A lasting case of déjà vu.
She was just someone I once met.

Is this the closest I shall get?
A missed rapport that I shall rue?
Ah she's a source of sweet regret.

I'm mystified by this onset
Of feeling love-struck, strange and blue.
She was just someone I once met.

'Infatuation', some would bet;
It couldn't be a love that's true.
But she's a source of sweet regret.

It sounds insane to say and yet
We may have made it, just us two.
She was just someone I once met,
But she's a source of sweet regret.

Michael E Ord

SOMEONE

In cold, damp earth where darkness stings
and single stars read lonely skies,
I watch the 'phone which never rings.

An open grave contorts my limbs
to unborn child; no stifled cries
in cold, damp earth where darkness stings.

Close to dreams, now Morpheus brings
someone to love. Behind closed eyes,
I watch the 'phone which never rings

and count the stars, the precious things,
warm fingertips; the truth of lies
in cold, damp earth where darkness stings.

I spread each dream beneath my wings.
Venus and Mars. In some surprise,
I watch the 'phone which never rings

and seal my tomb. The silence sings
a torch-song when the last star dies.
In cold, damp earth where darkness stings
I watch the 'phone which never rings.

Barbara L Richards

IN TIMES OF PEACE

How long will this internment last?
A tiny cell, the door shut tight.
Hostility has long-since passed.

Into this hell I have been cast.
The fading sun my only light.
How long will this internment last?

My hopes of freedom dying fast.
I couldn't hide, I had to fight.
Hostility has long-since passed.

With silent winds an icy blast
And tortured screams cry out at night.
How long with this internment last?

From day to day there's no contrast,
As murdered comrades haunt my sight.
Hostility has long-since passed.

The passing seconds feel so vast.
Eyes are blind to my hopeless plight.
How long will this internment last?
Hostility has long-since passed.

Carl Jones-Taylor

The Seas Of Strife

The waters of the floods of life
Burst out in one relentless sweep,
And borne upon the seas of strife.

'Tis only faith and firm belief
Can balance out this living brief,
The waters of the floods of life.

The sea its daily course must stride
With constant surge upon the reef,
And borne upon the seas of strife.

Come squall and shower, tempest rife
'Tis best to ride the calmer deep,
The waters of the floods of life.

'Tis wise to wait the storm's relief
To seek the haven's peaceful keep,
And borne upon the seas of strife.

The greatest storm the strong survive
There's never time to moan and weep,
The waters of the floods of life
And borne upon the seas of strife.

K C Thomas

TO WORK I GO DAY AFTER DAY

To work I go day after day,
So many years gone by,
To earn my pay, there surely is another way.

I'm on my bike day after day,
It's but a mile to work,
Oh how I wish for other ways to earn my pay.

Through office window day after day,
I watch the seasons come and go,
To earn my pay there surely is another way.

I think I'll leave, day after day,
I dream of walking out the door,
Oh how I wish for other ways to earn my pay.

I lose my nerve, day after day,
To pay my bills I need my wage,
To earn my pay there surely is another way.

So there I stay, day after day,
I wonder if I'll ever change,
Oh how I wish for other ways to earn my pay,
To earn my pay there surely is another way.

Juliette Blencowe

THE LONG SHADOWS

The long autumn shadows rise and fall
At eventide when day begins to close
Disappearing as the night is swift to call

Around us Heaven throws a purple shawl
Where the sky folds as the petals of a rose
The long autumn shadows rise and fall

Evening descends, the blood-red ball
Falters where the distant lazy river flows
Disappearing as the night is swift to call

Treetops impale defenceless sky so tall
In amber light where twisted foliage grows
The long autumn shadows rise and fall

Within the cooling earth creatures scratch and crawl
Hiding their secrets where only God knows
Disappearing as the night is swift to call

We lose ourselves in decay and urban sprawl
Far from where the north wind blows
The long autumn shadows rise and fall
Disappearing as the night is swift to call

Edward McErlane

THE HOUSE WAS GLOOMY AND GREY

It was quite alarming one grey day
As the house stood strange and still
Wishing I was far away

The house was bleak, old and grey
The wind cried a loud shrill
The time I went astray

The house was gloomy in a weird way
And stood on a desolate hill
Wishing I was far away

Glancing around on that fateful day
Bats landed on an old windowsill
The time I went astray

The house still haunts me, to my dismay
God knows the way I feel
Wishing I was far away

So, if you ever go to that house, I pray
It may give you a sensational thrill!
For, no one lived in that house full of decay
The time I went astray

Jean P McGovern

CALL OF THE WILD

Wings of prey catches one's eye
Standing tall and still
Spread out your wings and fly

Hover in the wind, adorn the sky
Proud and strong of will
Wings of prey catches one's eye

Search the land, seek from high
Sense your inner-skill
Spread out your wings and fly

Dark clouds form as time goes by
Life hears your piercing shrill
Wings of prey catches one's eye

Tension beckons, I must not lie
As you swoop to kill
Spread out your wings and fly

Your deed is done, we ask not why
Homeward bound to a distant hill
Wings of prey catches one's eye
Spread out your wings and fly

Kathleen Johnson

MY SPIRIT FLOATED CLOUD-LIKE O'ER THE EARTH

My spirit floated cloud-like o'er the earth,
Like fleecy clouds at heights of many miles,
As I looked down upon my place of birth.

At heights like these, of air there is a dearth;
But then I needed none, for all the whiles
My spirit floated cloud-like o'er the earth.

I looked back on my life; what was it worth?
Experiences came flooding back in piles,
As I looked down upon my place of birth.

I travelled southwards from a Scottish firth,
And saw a sight which filled my heart with smiles;
My spirit floated cloud-like o'er the earth.

I saw an ancient river, broad in girth,
And houses with their roofs of slate-grey tiles,
As I looked down upon my place of birth.

I saw in my old house a book of mirth
Once writ by me, my manuscripts in files.
My spirit floated cloud-like o'er the earth,
As I looked down upon my place of birth.

Roger Williams

CRIME DOESN'T PAY

Although they say crime doesn't pay
and tell me so, and tell me so,
I choose to think another way.

For have you never thought that they,
the barristers, have too much dough -
although they say crime doesn't pay?

And have you heard a bobby say
his take-home pay is much too low?
I choose to think another way.

There's Ronald Biggs snug tucked away
where British law can never go -
although they say crime doesn't pay.

My increased premium came today;
they think my sum insured too low.
I choose to think another way.

And so for all the victims pray
and watch the unsolved crime rate grow;
although they say crime doesn't pay
I choose to think another way.

Margaret Tufton

SHE WHO WOULD BE YOUR DAUGHTER-IN-LAW

Let no ill-feeling start
When first he speaks her name.
Stop . . . listen to your heart.

She rips your world apart;
You'll never be the same.
Let no ill-feeling start.

She plays her strumpet's part
And sets your boy aflame.
Stop . . . listen to your heart.

She flaunts her tempter's art.
Your boy is not to blame!
Let no ill-feeling start.

She's just a common tart!
The harlot has no shame!
Stop . . . listen to your heart.

Though she may wield the dart,
Yours is the prior claim.
Let no ill-feeling start.
Stop . . . listen to your heart.

Sheila White

DON'T LEND ME YOUR FEAR

If you are sincere
Know I chose this way.
Don't lend me your fear.

When dark shadows near
Lighten up the grey,
If you are sincere.

Though I shed a tear
Cause me no delay.
Don't lend me your fear.

Learn what I hold dear
And the price I'll pay,
If you are sincere.

When enemies jeer
And I hold them at bay
Don't lend me your fear.

When my own doubts rear -
When I feel dismay
If you are sincere
Don't lend me your fear.

R L Cooper

WHEN WILL YOU BE MINE?

Oh when, oh when, oh when will you be mine?
I know you love me more than you admit.
Remind me without words and I'll be fine.

I gaze at you intently as we dine
And find it hard, a yard apart, to sit.
Oh when, oh when, oh when will you be mine?

You do not say you love me, so I pine
For something to convince myself of it.
Remind me without words and I'll be fine.

And, if I pour my thoughts into my wine,
I'm bound to doubt and panic just a bit:
Oh when, oh when, oh when will you be mine?

But, when I'm out of sorts or out of line,
It doesn't mean I'm out of love - don't quit.
Remind me without words and I'll be fine.

Within your arms, I feel and taste each sign
Of sentiments your conscience won't permit.
Oh when, oh when, oh when will you be mine?
Remind me without words and I'll be fine.

Chris Young

TELL ME NOT OUR LOVE IS DEAD

Tell me not our love is dead
And we are now no more than friends.
Was it something that was said?

My love comes from heart and head,
That most worthiest of blends.
Tell me not our love is dead.

Now I walk with heavy tread,
Desperate to make amends.
Was it something that was said?

Threatened is the silken thread
On which my happiness depends.
Tell me not our love is dead.

Your silence turns my heart to lead,
In fear of that which it portends.
Was it something that was said?

I wait, consumed with darkest dread,
For you to voice the word that mends.
Tell me not our love is dead.
Was it something that was said?

F Jensen

THRENODY

It's suddenly so very still.
He came in from the snow and died.
He'd never thought to make a Will . . .

He'd never suffered, ne'er been ill.
The shock could never be denied.
It's suddenly so very still.

He little had save quest and quill
And piano which was all his pride.
He'd never thought to make a Will . . .

His laughter can no longer fill
The spaces twixt the times he sighed -
It's suddenly so very still.

His parting broke our hearts. Until
The dawn, incessantly we cried.
He'd never thought to make a Will . . .

Tho' spring smiles now on distant hill
And sun illumines countryside,
It's suddenly so very still.
He'd never thought to make a Will . . .

Susan Devlin

OCHAVANGA

We'd flown across the miles of endless sand,
At last the sight our eyes would long retain:
The green oasis was a treasure land.

Excitement mounting, eagerly we scanned
Lagoons, cool glades of trees where leopards reign.
We'd flown across the miles of endless sand

To see the buffalo, screw-horned eland
And elephants assembling after rain.
The green oasis was a treasure land:

Savannah grasses, lofty palms and stands
Of figs, tall reeds with groups of waving canes.
We'd flown across the miles of endless sand,

The beauty of the view well worth the rands
Which we'd been charged to hire our little plane.
The green oasis was a treasure land,

Our Ochavanga visit was long planned:
Lush delta in the Kalahari plain.
We'd flown across the miles of endless sand,
The green oasis was a treasure land.

Pam Russell

LEGACY

Almost forgotten the features wane
As years pass, memory often lies
Until in you they are seen again.

I think of them and what does remain?
The shape of mouth, the colour of eye?
Almost forgotten the features wane.

The essence is here, still strong and plain
Faces are hard to visualise
Until in you they are seen again.

You look like me, or am I too vain?
Age has produced a veiled disguise
Almost forgotten the features wane.

A new generation does maintain
The characteristics time denies
Until in you they are seen again.

Grandchildren, you show that extra gain
Lost love's looks leap evoking surprise
Almost forgotten the features wane
Until in you they are seen again.

Delphine Sym

EASTER SONG

Lift your voice in joyful tone,
Rejoice! Let hallelujahs ring,
And sing your praise to God alone.

Christ is risen, make it known,
All creation join and sing,
Lift your voice in joyful tone.

Rolled away is that great stone;
Ring out the bells, ding-dong-a-ding,
And sing your praise to God alone.

Let cymbals crash and bagpipes drone,
Trumpet, oboe, flute and string
Lift your voice in joyful tone.

God in His love has saved His own;
Come, bring a thankful offering
And sing your praise to God alone.

Christ did in death for sin atone,
Now in Heaven He reigns as King!
Lift your voice in joyful tone
And sing your praise to God alone.

Deirdre Rogers

WAKE, BEAUTIFUL ROSE

Wake, beautiful rose, from your winter's sleep.
Do not be afraid for springtime is near.
Free those petals from which your blossoms leap.

Display nature's beauty, hidden so deep.
Share with us the secrets that you hold dear.
Wake, beautiful rose, from your winter's sleep.

Let loose those buds before they grow too steep.
Open your heart, there is nothing to fear.
Free those petals from which your blossoms leap.

Those fragrant smells you can no longer keep.
Fill the air again, as you do each year.
Wake, beautiful rose, from your winter's sleep.

Birds and bees wait, for your harvest, to reap.
Those peaches and creams are now almost here.
Free those petals from which your blossoms leap.

Warmed is the earth from which you slowly creep.
The world is ready for you to appear.
Wake, beautiful rose, from your winter's sleep.
Free those petals from which your blossoms leap.

David Barrow

TREAT THE GIRL

Please treat the girl with courtesy,
When she dreams that she can fly
She's lost within her fantasy.

She needs the sense of privacy
As her fears are kissed goodbye,
Please treat the girl with courtesy.

Some would call it lunacy,
Can't see the reason why
She's lost within her fantasy.

She guards her dreams with jealousy
Won't let you see her cry,
Please treat the girl with courtesy.

As she's wrapped in spiritual ecstasy,
You simply can't deny
She's lost within her fantasy.

When her mood is that of poignancy
You'll hear her wistful sigh,
Please treat the girl with courtesy
She's lost within her fantasy.

Sally Malone

BUZZING LIFE IN OUR CITIES

Old men and women carrying heavy bags,
        as the smart cars go whizzing by.
- These are our pensioners' (*medal*) tags!

Shrieks from kids who call them hags,
        they struggle on without a sigh.
- Old men and women carrying heavy bags.

What matters if their body sags?
        they soldier on, and do not cry.
- These are our pensioners' (*medal*) tags!

People ignore the loads he drags,
        he's one of them! - (with just one eye),
- Old men and women carrying heavy bags.

At crowded bus-stops amongst cans and fags,
        she hopes the bus will soon come by,
- These are our pensioners' (*medal*) tags!

For them, life's ending, the time just lags,
        as they silently stand, waiting to die,
Old men and women carrying heavy bags;
- These are our pensioners' (*medal*) tags!

Beatrice Wilson

CHILDHOOD'S MOUNTAINS

My childhood's mountains round the lake today,
Made real at last, not wishful fantasy;
They haunted me when I was far away.

Here now, I need not search in dreams for them. They
Are no longer seen through mists of memory,
My childhood's mountains round the lake today.

I look at cloaks of snow and sunlight, at grey
And bony fingers, that point up ruggedly.
They haunted me when I was far away.

The people I have loved have gone. I stay
A stranger in this place now. - But I can see
My childhood's mountains round the lake today.

They do not change, whatever else here may.
My friendly giants are as they used to be. -
They haunted me when I was far away.

While I look back, as I come home, they play
Their part: parents and daughter, they comfort me,
My childhood's mountains round the lake today. -
They haunted me when I was far away.

T Agnes McCaig

BURIED TREASURE

In the beginning, long before time began,
When faith, and hope and love were as yet unborn,
The creation was planned and perfected by the Divine.

And from God's inner being, before dim ageless ages,
Emerged eternal truth, made strong with in-built endurance,
In the beginning, long before time began.

And God then made man, and from his far beginnings
Man mislaid silence, and spouted words endlessly. But
The creation was planned and perfected by the Divine.

And though man piles endless words upon endless searing words,
Truth transfixed in his soul seeks to escape to what once was,
In the beginning, long before time began.

But words still spew out in endless spate, submerging that
Which the Master Craftsman implanted at the core of man's heart, when
The creation was planned and perfected by the Divine.

And when man looks deep down into the depths of his soul
He cannot see the truth within, but is sure it was there
In the beginning. Long before time began
The creation was planned and perfected by the Divine!

Dan Pugh

ONLY SKIN DEEP

I say to all those who lust after me,
'Though I may please your partial eye,
I have other qualities that you cannot see.'

'Do not be misled by simple physical beauty,
For that is not where my real talents lie,'
I say to all those who lust after me.

Though born into that half of our gender tree
Defined by its paucity of chromosomal 'Y',
I have other qualities that you cannot see.

'But how can I convey intellectual capacity,
With this body over which so many sigh?'
I say to all those who lust after me.

Yet, I do so need to be taken seriously,
That even my very soul is beginning to cry,
'I have other qualities that you cannot see!'

And therefore, because I seek an identity
That will survive when beauty begins to die,
I say to all those who lust after me,
'I have other qualities that you cannot see!'

Andrew Farmer

That Knowing Look

I feel that she's the adult, I'm the child.
My little girl, now knowing all,
Just looked at me and smiled.

Now she has the boys beguiled,
A beauty, proud and tall,
I feel that she's the adult, I'm the child.

She's always sensible, not wild,
rebuked me often I recall,
Just looked at me and smiled.

She's even-tempered, never riled,
placid whate'er may befall.
I feel that she's the adult, I'm the child.

Her hair's the same, simply styled,
as when she, a toddler small,
Just looked at me and smiled.

I said that somehow, in life's file,
our order is reversed and overall,
I feel that she's the adult, I'm the child.
She just looked at me and smiled.

Sylvia J Wilkinson

THE GARDEN

Into the garden you must go
Enjoy the sun or summer's breeze
Spade in hand, rake or hoe

Cutting hedges, lawns to mow
The wind blows gently through the trees
Into the garden, you must go

Attending plants, seeds to sow
Aching legs through bending knees
Spade in hand, rake or hoe

A fruitless task with weeds that grow
Every opportunity, we always seize
Into the garden, you must go

Beads of sweat form and flow
Time to rest and stand at ease
Spade in hand, rake or hoe

Results achieved when seedlings show
Slugs and snails will start to tease
Into the garden you must go
Spade in hand, rake or hoe.

Dennis N Davies

MONKEY BUSINESS

The higher the monkey climbs the tree
The more he shows his tail
We see how devious he can be

Suppressing thoughts of honesty
The opportunist will prevail
The higher the monkey climbs the tree

With vigilance we're sure to see
The tricks played by the cunning male
We see how devious he can be

Cares not a jot for loyalty
He's arrogant, his soul's for sale
The higher the monkey climbs the tree

But as he climbs we all agree
He leaves a bitter trail
We see how devious he can be

So we who stand beneath the tree
His misdemeanours should unveil
The higher the monkey climbs the tree
We see how devious he can be.

June Plange

FAMINE AND WAR

Relentless sun, earth scorched, no haven there to hide
Their skeletal frame, silent, sombre fear,
We see it now, we saw it then and cried.

Land cracked and dry, no harvest yield supplied,
No miracle of loaves and fishes here,
They hunger now, they hungered then and died.

War's strident sound meets famine, they collide
In conflict, helpless, hopeless, homeless sphere,
We see it now, we saw it then and cried.

Humility in eye that lessens not a pride
Of bearing, sit in dignity of years,
They hunger now, they hungered then and died.

Milk-starved, fly-covered, hands clutching breasts - dried,
Images on a screen, they vanish, clear,
We see it now, we saw it then and cried.

Shadows of holocausts' past cry out - denied!
Was mankind listening, watching, learning here.
We see it now, we saw it then and cried,
They hunger now, they hungered then and died.

Jean Bishop

GERIATRIC RECONCILIATION

I doubt I'll ever be a famous man;
I'm old in years and soft in brain today.
Is it too bad to be an also-ran?

I've seldom done those things which laws do ban
And I have done my best and had my say.
I doubt I'll ever be a famous man.

Two stalwart sons do better than I can
In many things involved in work and play.
Is it too bad to be an also-ran?

Although I've had my moments in life's plan
Which won some plaudits and the odd hurray,
I doubt I'll ever be a famous man.

Few deeds did earn those words, éclat, élan;
Were I a god I would have feet of clay.
Is it too bad to be an also-ran?

One thing stands out since my review began;
My striving brought much fun along the way.
I doubt I'll ever be a famous man.
Is it too bad to be an also-ran?

F Sutton

EARLY RISERS

The blush of dawn illuminates the skies -
Morning mist, a wraith upon the moor,
Before our infant son awakes and cries.

Below, hot bacon sizzles as it fries.
Temptation gets me out of bed before
The blush of dawn illuminates the skies.

The clock ticks on. The fleeting hour flies.
I listen for your tap upon the door
Before our infant son awakes and cries.

I fold your gown, adorned with butterflies.
Sunlight spills across the bedroom floor.
The blush of dawn illuminates the skies.

The omelette spits. Fumes begin to rise.
Strong tea, well brewed, in mugs we pour,
Before our infant son awakes and cries.

Your voice is soft, but softer still, your sighs.
Beneath bright, cotton sheets we slip once more.
The blush of dawn illuminates the skies,
Before our infant son awakes and cries.

Pauline Pullan

REMEMBRANCE DAY

Flowers on the graves
On this Remembrance Day,
For those who died to save.

Boys too young to shave
Their lives not underway,
Flowers on the graves.

Sent off with smiles and waves,
By crowds that cheered 'Hurray,'
For those who died to save.

Jingoistic verver made them brave
For the part they had to play,
Flowers on the graves.

Their fear they tried to stave
A time to learn to pray,
For those who died to save.

So as a nation we cannot waive
In our responsibility to lay,
Flowers on the graves
For those who died to save.

Keith Tissington

FLORIDA RAIN

Stood still, embraced in sheets of Florida rain,
Water curtains falling upon vistas stricken blind;
Where humid tears may yet be shed again.

Terminal concourse swathed in loss and pain,
Blurring out of sight yet clear in mind;
Stood still, embraced in sheets of Florida rain.

Bowed heads in knowing full that never the 'twain
Shall meet, nor ever more these souls will find
Where humid tears may yet be shed again.

Should alligator jaws from foaming drain
Feast on the last of love that stays behind,
Stood still, embraced in sheets of Florida rain?

Storm clouds in the heart and in the brain
Turn darker now than Mother Nature's kind,
Where humid tears may yet be shed again.

If only there were some way to obtain
A means by which such love could be enshrined,
Stood still, embraced in sheets of Florida rain
Where humid tears may yet be shed again.

Tony Bush

THE KITE

The kite soars on high,
Tails whisper and dance,
Like a bird in the sky.

I feel I can fly,
If I just had the chance,
The kite soars on high.

Planes fly slowly by,
Barely giving a glance,
Like a bird in the sky.

Children laugh clap and sigh,
While friends look on askance,
The kite soars on high.

What bonds I could tie,
If I learned how to prance,
Like a bird in the sky.

But the dance has to die,
The string swoops in a trance,
The kite soars on high,
Like a bird in the sky . . .

Margaret W Farrand

LEAVE TAKING

What happens when true love dies?
Frail emotions torn apart;
When you only see two faithless eyes.

Betrayal, hurt and many lies,
Have replaced the days of joy;
What happens when true love dies?

A laugh a smile a mere disguise,
To hide the torment deep inside,
When you only see two faithless eyes.

The breaking heart is no surprise,
The trust of years now all destroyed;
What happens when true love dies?

The parting means no bonds, no ties,
Hard to take the pain you feel,
When you only see two faithless eyes.

The empty hours of tears and sighs,
You try to accept this bitter loss;
What happens when true love dies?
When you only see two faithless eyes.

A L Manning

SUCH A DOG'S VACATION!

Such is a dog's vacation,
Country kennels, when owners go abroad.
Out of sight, out of mind - no consideration!

Meals are served on a tray, plenty of time for meditation.
Accommodation is small and smelly.
Such is a dog's vacation!

Surrounded by rolls of wire, strangers try to be kind.
They can bark all day, till hoarse.
Out of sight, out of mind!

The dogs suffer depression, desertion, with no limitation,
Wondering why they are being punished this way.
Such is a dog's vacation!

While their owners have a good time,
Their best friend is facing a plight.
Out of sight, out of mind!

The dog has no choice, but to suffer frustration.
No wonder, they don't like suitcases.
Such is a dog's vacation!
Out of sight, out of mind without consideration.

Annemarie Poole

WISHFUL THINKING

I look in the mirror and what do I see
Standing there gazing, perfectly still,
Why, it's only my familiar face gazing out at me.

Realistically looking I let fantasy be
You're standing behind me, a real thrill,
But why do I only see me, not thee?

I gaze long and hard, one, two, should become three
You're not there, it's only me again and no darling dog Bill,
Why, it's only my familiar face gazing out at me.

Two more beings looking deep in the mirror with me
Standing in line with soldier skill,
But why do I only see me, not thee?

I'm having great trouble seeing both you two
There's neither thee nor darling dog Bill,
Why, it's only my familiar face gazing out at me.

Just seeing you two was not to be
You're both long gone over the hill,
I look in the mirror and what do I see
Why, it's only my familiar face gazing out at me.

M C Hornby

To RWB

I miss you in the morning
I hear the blackbird sing
Friend comforter of mine

Two pressed flowers, a handkerchief
Are all that I can see
I miss you in the morning.

You could make me laugh
Said your shoes were ingots of lead
Friend comforter of mine.

You took me back in time
Sitting by your bed, it was Easter
I miss you in the morning.

We listened to music together
I sang the old songs for you
Friend comforter of mine

The last few weeks you suffered
A raised eyebrow, a glint of eye of blue
I miss you in the morning
Friend comforter of mine.

Anne Seymour

BRAVE WALLACE - 1297

Brave Wallace knew the time was nigh
to rout the enemy, maim and kill -
knew his men were ready, standing by.

He realised they could no longer lie
in wait up there upon the hill -
Brave Wallace knew the time was nigh

to descend to Stirling Bridge, to try
to halt the enemy, advancing still -
knew his men were ready, standing by.

Each man, eager, ready, too, to die,
and English blood to spill -
Brave Wallace knew the time was nigh.

He fought hard, saw the English turn and fly
away in panic - felt the battle thrill,
knew his men were ready, standing by.

It was a glorious victory, aye,
that Scots remember still -
Brave Wallace *knew* the time was nigh -
knew his men were ready, standing by.

Joyce Hockley

IMMORTAL

I hear my father, kind and wise.
Inspiring words heard long ago
echo feelings, soften my eyes.

I embrace my father, he dries
my tears. Tender care stems the flow.
I hear my father kind and wise.

I hold my father's hand; he dies
beyond reproach, and songs I know
echo feelings, soften my eyes.

I see his bent frame; he tries
to remain tall until we grow.
I hear my father kind and wise.

I sense his strong presence; he'll rise
immortal. Drifts of love follow,
echo feelings, soften my eyes.

He rests in my heart, hears my sighs,
pilots the ship, when ill winds blow.
I hear my father, kind and wise,
echo feelings, soften my eyes.

Maureen Bold

My Happiness Has Left Me

My happiness has left me,
The day you went far away,
And I'm as sad as can be.

Happy times we had, all free,
Until you were lead astray.
My happiness has left me.

But why, did you have to flee,
Now my life seems in decay,
And I'm as sad as can be.

To my heart, you had a key,
My secret love, you did betray.
My happiness has left me.

You just ignored my own plea,
I wanted you to delay,
And I'm as sad as can be.

But time will heal, wait and see,
I may forget you some day.
My happiness has left me,
And I'm as sad as can be.

D M L Ranson

THE JIGSAW

A jigsaw vast the Master made
and sent it down to earth,
a vivid cavalcade was laid

an intricately wrought brocade
of joy and precious worth.
A jigsaw vast the Master made

with colours that shall never fade;
of richness there's no dearth.
A vivid cavalcade was laid,

its jewels ceaselessly cascade
upon a heedless earth.
A jigsaw vast the Master made,

a never-ending rich parade
to please his creatures on the earth
a vivid cavalcade was laid.

Our grateful thanks are oft delayed
for glory of such heavenly birth.
A jigsaw vast the Master made,
a vivid cavalcade was laid.

Geraldine Squires

SEXUAL FEAR

Please don't touch me
Please don't try
Can't you see?

Leave me be
Go away
Please don't touch me

I'm not happy
With you here
Can't you see?

We're not 'we'
I'm not with you
Please don't touch me

Turn that key
Back again
Can't you see?

Set me free
Do what's right
Please don't touch me
Can't you see?

Sonia Richards

H, H, H, H.

Tell me, what are they laughing for?
When the comedian is dead,
Nothing seems funny anymore.

Why then do they try to laugh more?
With laughter farthest from my head,
Tell me, what are they laughing for?

Should I laugh as well, I'm not sure,
Is it tears or laughter I dread?
Nothing seems funny anymore.

I've heard the jokes, I know the score,
Now I've completely lost the thread,
Tell me, what are they laughing for?

Is the answer those clothes he wore?
Or that look, or something he said,
Nothing seems funny anymore.

The jester is dead, I've said before,
I've shared the tears that have been shed,
Tell me, what are they laughing for?
Nothing seems funny anymore.

Peter Chaney

YOUR BAD DREAM

You must not cry
What's this I hear?
Please wipe your eye

With trembling lip you give a sigh
I brush away your tear
You must not cry

Can you explain, tell me why
What is it that you fear?
Please wipe your eye

A welcome smile was your reply
From rumpled bed you peer
You must not cry

Mouse-like acting very shy
Whispered troubles make it clear
Please wipe your eye

With love I calm and pacify
Let your bad dream disappear
You must not cry
Please wipe your eye.

E Jones

THE LEAVES OF THE WILLOW

The leaves are green upon the willow tree
Forget the empty fronds - the winter's snow.
Look at them now - those who have eyes to see.

See how the spring-grown tufts dance airily,
While wind-blown petals from the fruit-trees flow.
The leaves are green upon the willow tree;

Consider not what things are yet to be,
When the last blossoms from their anchors go.
Look at them now - those who have eyes to see,

When summer's heat drives everyone to flee
For soothing shade, they will be glad to know
The leaves are green upon the willow tree.

Autumn's first frosts will strike relentlessly
And limp brown corpses strew the turf below.
Look at them now - those who have eyes to see.

There will be times when winds blow icily
And minds forget the springs of long ago.
The leaves are green upon the willow tree.
Look at them *now* - those who have eyes to see.

Eric Dixon

WILL WE MEET AGAIN?

Will we meet again
When all the world's at peace
When sunshine follows rain?

What memories remain
When faculties decrease
Will we meet again?

Will anyone explain
Will powers of evil cease
When sunshine follows rain?

One's loss another's gain
Where is the Golden Fleece
Will we meet again?

What dreams we entertain
In our wild caprice
When sunshine follows rain.

Will moons still wax and wane
And will our love increase
Will we meet again
When sunshine follows rain?

Edward C Fairweather

DEATH'S DRUM

How keen the thoughts of our mortality become,
How sharp the inner whisper of life's nearing end,
When we have heard the muffled beating of death's drum.

And when we calculate life's bill, knowing its sum
Is fixed - in this we cannot borrow, cannot lend -
How keen the thoughts of our mortality become.

Shout your frustration! Shriek it! But the words that come
We know cannot deny the truth, so why pretend,
When we have heard the muffled beating of death's drum?

Why waste breath? Save it for the life that's left. Why plumb
The depths? Who has not heard it cannot comprehend
How keen the thoughts of our mortality become.

Take heart. Believe. Deny those thoughts which seek to numb
The hope - on which our sure and present lives depend -
When we have heard the muffled beating of death's drum;

And know it matters not, if we do not succumb -
If we remember to embrace life as a friend -
How keen the thoughts of our mortality become,
When we have heard the muffled beating of death's drum.

Brian Travis

THE JOURNEY ONWARD

Do not be sad because the time draws near
To bid a farewell to my earthly stay.
The journey onward knows no lasting fear

For one whose course beyond this life will steer
To sunsets where the fleeting shadows play.
Do not be sad because the time draws near

To walk an unknown tideline and to hear
The echoes of eternal yesterday.
The journey onward knows no lasting fear

That I shall lose the music of the sphere,
The breaking waves, to guide me on my way.
Do not be sad because the time draws near

To contemplate, to ponder, and revere
Life's amaranthine caravanserai;
The journey onward knows no lasting fear.

The memories of all that I hold dear
Will comfort me along my lonesome way;
Do not be sad because the time draws near,
The journey onward knows no lasting fear.

Grahame Godsmark

A MOUNTAIN MYSTERY

In all my days, I never seem to know,
Despite the fascination and the fears,
Why mountains in a mist should move me so.

Why jagged peaks where cloudy veils hang low
Should be my inspiration down the years,
In all my days, I never seem to know.

In April, when their rainbow waters flow,
I wonder, while their song delights my ears,
Why mountains in a mist should move me so.

In summer through a golden haze they show,
And why their majesty my spirit cheers,
In all my days, I never seem to know.

In winter, when they loom through swirling snow,
I ponder, as each ghostly peak appears,
Why mountains in a mist should move me so.

Their beauty sets my questing heart aglow,
And, though it brings me to the edge of tears,
In all my days, I never seem to know
Why mountains in a mist should move me so.

Brenda G Macrow

ON THE STREET

Don't look at me like that as you pass by,
I did not ask to live here on the street
Shed not your tears for me if I should die.

A park bench is the bed whereon I lie,
With stiffly aching limbs and frozen feet.
Don't look at me like that as you pass by.

For cash hand-outs I do not qualify,
'No fixed abode' does not criteria meet.
Shed not your tears for me if I should die.

To you I'm just a dirty, unkempt guy,
A scrounger, begging every bite I eat.
Don't look at me like that as you pass by.

How lonely is the world for such as I,
How lucky you, who are of the elite
Shed not your tears for me if I should die.

You look at me with contempt in your eye,
Not caring if I starve here on the street,
Don't look at me like that as you pass by,
Shed not your tears for me if I should die.

Mary Fleming

GOD IS LOVE

God is love, man's hope despite his errant ways
Eschewing it in soulless stride,
Cries out at fading of his fleeting days.

Created, but to bask in ephem'ral rays
First - Adam fell, whilst angels cried
'God is love,' man's hope despite his errant ways.

Unique the heart, matchless love and endless grace
Flowed on. And man, his need denied
Cries out at fading of his fleeting days.

Still, stark tree, mute witness of satanic gaze
Saw sin's recoil prove death defied.
God is love. Man's hope despite his errant ways.

Pentecostal morn' and faith now God repays
With pow'r anew. Man sanctified
Cries out at fading of his fleeting days.

Fading days now live! A freedom song to raise
Proclaims to all whose flame has died,
'God is love!' Man's hope, despite his errant ways
Cries out at fading of his fleeting days.

Fred Croudace

LOST YOUTH

I sigh, and turn a page
as bitter winter chills.
Oh, that I need not age.

But after winter's rage
appear the daffodils.
I sigh; and turn a page.

Their beauty is a gauge
of what, in nature, thrills.
Oh, that I need not age.

For then I could engage
with sporting Jacks and Jills.
I sigh; and turn a page.

From my imprisoning cage
I contemplate my ills.
Oh, that I need not age.

While youngsters take the stage
and I resort to pills
I sigh; and turn a page
Oh, that I need not age.

Grace Mills

How May We Judge . . . ?

How may we judge the pattern of the years?
Nine decades like the passing of a dream,
A living tapestry of hopes and fears?

Such change as in one lifetime's span appears,
Its forebears scarcely tuned to air and steam -
How may we judge the pattern of the years?

The loving home, the soon-forgotten tears,
The laughing days, in retrospect will seem
A living tapestry of hopes and fears.

No earlier generation's progress cheers
Or chills like this: thus rapid, thus extreme,
How may we judge the pattern of the years?

And year by pulsing year a lifetime steers
Our unregarding steps to trace this stream,
A living tapestry of hopes and fears.

Too close to comprehend stark truth appears.
Wisdom or cleverness: which proves supreme?
How may we judge the pattern of the years,
A living tapestry of hopes and fears?

Kathleen M Hatton

IN YOUR BLUE FIFTIES DRESS

In your blue fifties dress,
I thought I saw you there,
And now I cannot rest.

I'm remembering the best;
You, wondrous and fair,
In your blue fifties dress.

How did we manage this mess?
We lost a love so rare,
And now I cannot rest.

Time was our personal caress;
We danced, and you with flair,
In your blue fifties dress.

Children were ours, oh bliss, oh bless,
But they believed I did not care,
And now I cannot rest.

The signal I send is me in distress,
I need to see you everywhere -
In your blue fifties dress;
And now I cannot rest.

Pauline Nash

TREATS FOR THE YEAR 2000

Now, a millennium's approaching, and junketings are planned:
Indeed, London is to have a spanking new, plastic Dome
To honour the occasion. Construction is in hand

By the river. Though the chosen site's polluted land,
It is to be rendered safe by decontaminating foam,
Now a millennium's approaching, and junketings are planned.

A spin doctor is in charge of the project, and has scanned
Many hundred of suggestions as to how to fill the Dome
To honour the occasion. Construction is in hand.

Though lambasted by the critics, he has taken a firm stand
Against overtly Christian exhibits. Aware that this seems rum
Now a millennium's approaching, and junketings are planned,

He claims that, to ensure that queues of visitors are manned
By hordes of eager punters, who just cannot wait to come
To honour the occasion (construction *is* in hand),

Marvels modern must predominate o'er means to make
                                        them understand
What 'A.D.' stands for. He'll leave that task to the Church of Rome,
Now a millennium's approaching, and junketings are planned
To honour the occasion. Construction is in hand!

Jean M Bell

SARAJEVO 1993

birds gape from the nest; empty mouths to be fed
as fire blossoms out from the hills
she takes her life in her hands with a loaf of bread

rubble the home, crumpled iron the bed,
quietly in dusk a neighbour his neighbour kills
birds gape from the nest; empty mouths to be fed

school is closed; the children who sang are fled
the sun in the west warms no longer but chills
she takes her life in her hands with a loaf of bread

no peace in the grave for the lucky dead
murder peers over frayed windowsills
birds gape from the nest; empty mouths to be fed

the wounded man has stone to cradle his head
scattering for cover as the lifeblood spills
she takes her life in her hands with a loaf of bread

the past forgotten, the future weighs like lead
torture and threats directed by human wills
birds gape from the nest; empty mouths to be fed
she takes her life in her hands with a loaf of bread

Sheila Smith

THE AGE OF AQUARIUS

Aquarius enters in a towering rage;
Slams the gently closing old year's door,
Makes his presence felt upon the stage

Where Neptune with Uranus will engage,
Letting loose the mighty dogs of war.
Aquarius enters in a towering rage,

And, careless now, in thunderous rampage
Empties his libation on Earth's floor;
Makes his presence felt upon the stage,

Heralds in that fabled golden age,
Watched for with anxiety and awe.
Aquarius enters in a towering rage,

And change is there, on every living page.
But will he leave us better than before?
He makes his presence felt upon the stage,

But does he come to ravage or assuage?
And will we find the pain is worth the cure?
Aquarius enters in a towering rage,
Makes his presence felt upon the stage.

Kit Jackson

PASTORALE

(The story goes that the young Benjamin Franklin, while in Paris,
was continually scorned by scholars because of his belief in the Bible.
So he called them together and read them the Book of Ruth . . .)

'Intreat me not to leave you, nor forsake . . .'
Ben Franklin faced the bigots who ridiculed him sore -
'Whatever road you follow I will take.'

Deciding that some gesture he must make
To shield the treasured Book whose faith he bore . . .
'Intreat me not to leave you, nor forsake . . .'

For he could not suffer endless taunts of 'Fake!'
So called his ridiculers, two, three, four . . .
'Whatever road you follow I will take . . .'

'I bid you listen to this tale prosaic . . .'
They heard, and hearing clamoured, 'More!'
'Intreat me not to leave you, nor forsake.'

They saw its publication was at stake -
Such love and loyalty never known before -
'Whatever road you follow I will take.'

Ben Franklin laughed so much that he should break
Their criticisms hoarded by the score.
'Intreat me not to leave you, nor forsake,
Whatever road you follow I will take.'

Patricia Batstone

THE FUNNY LITTLE CAR

I bought a funny little car,
Its colour was bright green,
In it I will go far.

I took it round to show my pa,
Said he, 'The likes of it I have never seen
It looks just like a jar.'

'Well!' said I, 'To me it's a star
And no matter where its been
In it I will go far.'

Then I showed it to my ma,
She said, 'Be careful where you lean,
It looks just like a jar. '

To them it may look peculiar,
Inside it they would never be seen,
In it I will go far.

Well, think of me wherever you are,
For it goes smoothly as a dream
It looks just like a jar,
In it I will go far.

Maud Eleanor Hobbs